GREAT BRITONS

CAMPAIGNERS
for CHANGE

Ann Kramer

FRANKLIN WATTS
LONDON•SYDNEY

First published in 2007 by
Franklin Watts

Copyright © Franklin
Watts 2007

Franklin Watts
338 Euston Road
London NW1 3BH

Franklin Watts Australia
Level 17/207 Kent Street
Sydney, NSW 2000

A CIP catalogue record for
this book is available from
the British Library.

Dewey number: 920.02

ISBN: 978 0 7496 7475 5

Printed in China

Franklin Watts is a division
of Hachette Children's
Books.

Designer: Thomas Keenes
Art Director: Jonathan Hair
Editor: Sarah Ridley
Editor-in-Chief:
John C. Miles
Picture Research:
Diana Morris

Picture credits:
AP/Topfoto: 35, 41. Mary
Evans Picture Library: 27.
Fortean Picture Library/
Topfoto: 29. Fotomas/
Topfoto: 24-25.
National Pictures/Topfoto:
45. PA/Topham: 38.
Picturepoint/Topham: 7, 9,
12, 15, 17, 18, 21, 31, 36,
42-43. Roger-Viollet/
Topfoto: 11. Ann Ronan
Picture Library/HIP/
Topfoto: 22. Topfoto: front
cover, 32.

Every attempt has been made to
clear copyright. Should there be
any inadvertent omission please
apply to the publisher for
rectification.

CONTENTS

INTRODUCTION

Throughout British history, women and men have stood up, challenged society and campaigned for change. Some have worked alone, others as part of a political party or campaigning group. All have aimed to tackle injustice and change society for the better, often against terrible opposition.

Twenty of these great campaigners are included in this book. Many campaigned to achieve civil liberties, such as the right to vote in elections and equal rights of citizenship that we take for granted today. Getting the vote did not just happen. It was a long hard struggle, stretching way back to the 17th century. Without campaigners such as John Lilburne, William Lovett and Emmeline Pankhurst, whose stories are told here, we might never have had the vote for all. Mary Wollstonecraft kick-started women's rights and Lord David Pitt fought tirelessly against racism.

Other campaigners in this book fought to combat sickness, poverty and exploitation. They include Elizabeth Fry who reformed prisons, Edwin Chadwick who led politicians to make improvements in public health, Lord Shaftesbury who protected child workers, Ellen Wilkinson who marched for the unemployed and Eleanor

Rathbone who brought in the idea of child benefit.

Threats to our lives do not disappear. More recent campaigners included here are Jonathan Porritt, who has highlighted the environmental dangers facing us all, and Shami Chakrabati, who has campaigned to keep hard-won civil liberties.

You, of course, will have your own favourite campaigners, and will wonder why some of them are not in this book. A list such as this is always personal, and can always be changed with good reason. But it is true to say that each and every person in this book changed the course of British history in one way or another, and has left their mark for future generations to study, and admire.

JOHN WYCLIFFE
PRIEST AND CHURCH REFORMER

BORN Yorkshire,
c. 1324
DIED Lutterworth,
Leicestershire,
31 December 1384

John Wycliffe (also spelled Wyclif) challenged the power and wealth of the medieval Church. His views were years ahead of their time and very influential. After his death, his ideas spread and paved the way for the English Reformation in 1534 and the growth of Protestantism.

Wycliffe studied and taught divinity (religious studies) at Oxford University. In about 1373 he became rector (a type of priest) at Lutterworth, Leicestershire. At the time, the Catholic Church was the only Christian Church in medieval Europe. Headed by the Pope in Rome, it was rich and powerful and owned vast estates. It regulated people's everyday lives and played a leading role in government.

From about 1374, Wycliffe began speaking out against the wealth and power of the Church. He believed the Church had moved too far from the teachings of Christ and had lost touch with ordinary people. He criticised Church leaders and challenged the authority of the Pope and the archbishops. He said that the Bible and its teachings should be available to all, not just the clergy. Wycliffe believed the

The Lollards

Wycliffe's followers were called Lollards, from a Dutch word meaning 'mumbler'. They were poor priests who travelled the country spreading Wycliffe's ideas. Under his instruction, some of them translated the Bible from Latin into English, so that more people could read it. Their attacks on the corruption of the Church won them support from the poor and the nobility. However, it was a crime, known as heresy, to criticise Church teachings and in 1401 parliament passed a law allowing heretics to be burnt to death. Following a Lollard uprising in 1414, many were burned alive. The movement receded but continued into the 16th century.

Church should be stripped of wealth, which should be used for the poor. Luckily, he had some powerful friends who protected him. However, when Wycliffe criticised the Holy Communion, the Church hit back and banned his writings. He retired to Lutterworth but escaped punishment. After his death, the Church declared him a heretic. His ideas, however, lived on. 🏴󠁧󠁢󠁥󠁮󠁧󠁿

John Wycliffe's writings paved the way for the English Reformation.

JOHN LILBURNE
POLITICAL LEADER AND WRITER

BORN Greenwich, London c. 1614
DIED Eltham, Kent, 29 August 1657

Sometimes known as 'Freeborn John', John Lilburne was one of the great heroes of the English Civil War. More than 300 years ago, he was one of the first to demand that all men should have the vote in elections. He was imprisoned many times for such revolutionary ideas.

Lilburne was born into a fairly wealthy family. He was apprenticed in the cloth trade, and as a young man became interested in politics. In 1638 he was publicly whipped and imprisoned for distributing Puritan pamphlets, which was forbidden. In 1642 civil war broke out between parliament and the king, Charles I, over who should govern the country. Lilburne, by now free again, joined the parliamentary army, later known as the New Model Army. He was a brave fighter.

In 1645 the parliamentarians, led by Oliver Cromwell, gained victory over the king, who was imprisoned. A new political group emerged, known as the Levellers. Inspired by Lilburne, they believed that all men, whether rich or poor, should have the vote. This was unheard of because at that time only landowners could have a say in government. Cromwell and other parliamentarians intended to rule the country: they were horrified at the idea that ordinary men might vote. It was not what Cromwell had intended.

In 1647 Lilburne and other Leveller leaders were arrested. From his prison cell, Lilburne continued to demand change. His ideas spread like wildfire, particularly among ordinary soldiers. There were debates between Cromwell and army representatives but Cromwell had no intention of acting on their demands. In 1649 the king was executed, England became a republic and Cromwell was eventually made Lord Protector. Lilburne was arrested and sent to prison in Jersey. He was imprisoned again for two years when he returned to England. At the end of his life he became a Quaker and died of fever at the age of 42. Gradually the Leveller movement faded away but its ideas inspired later political movements.

THOMAS (TOM) PAINE
REVOLUTIONARY AND WRITER

BORN Thetford, Norfolk, 29 January 1737
DIED New York, United States, 8 June 1809

Tom Paine was the most revolutionary and influential political writer of his time. He supported the American and French revolutions, attacked the British monarchy, and called for radical political change. He was considered so dangerous in Britain that he was outlawed.

Paine led an adventurous life. From the age of 13 he worked in many jobs, as a corset maker, sailor and teacher. For a while he was a customs and excise man in Lewes, Sussex, but was sacked after he wrote a pamphlet calling for higher wages.

In 1774, Paine went to America, then part of the British Empire, where he worked as a political journalist, writing articles on topics such as women's rights and the abolition of slavery. In 1775 he wrote a pamphlet, *Common Sense*, urging American independence from Britain. It was enormously influential. Some 500,000 Americans read it and its wording was used in the Declaration of Independence (1776). He fought alongside the American rebels and wrote leaflets and pamphlets to keep up their spirits. In one of these he coined the phrase 'United States of America'.

In 1787 Paine returned to England. Following the outbreak of the French Revolution, he wrote his most famous book, *The Rights of Man* (1791). In this he not only defended the French Revolution, but also attacked the British monarchy and aristocracy, called for a republic and demanded social changes such as old age pensions, support for the poor and taxation of the rich. Terrified that revolution would spread to Britain, the government demanded his

Revolutionary times

The late 18th century was a revolutionary time. Between 1774-83, American colonists fought for, and won, independence from Britain. Between 1789-92, revolutionaries in France overthrew the monarchy, executed the royal family and declared a republic.

arrest for treason and made it against the law to buy or read his work.

Paine fled to France where he was welcomed and joined the National Convention. But in 1793 he found himself in a French prison for opposing the execution of the King of France. While in prison, he wrote *Age of Reason*, an attack on religion. He was released from prison in 1794 and, as he was forbidden from returning to Britain, he travelled to the United States where he died in poverty. By the time of his death, over a million people had read *Age of Reason*.

Paine's revolutionary views influenced the founding fathers of the United States.

MARY WOLLSTONECRAFT
EARLY FEMINIST AND WRITER

BORN Spitalfields, London, 27 April 1759
DIED London, 10 September 1797

Mary Wollstonecraft was an outspoken feminist at a time when women were supposed to be quiet, gentle and obedient to men. Her book, *A Vindication of the Rights of Women*, is often considered to be the starting point for feminism, the fight for equal rights for women, in Britain.

A portrait of Mary Wollstonecraft, whose book marked a starting point for feminism.

Mary Wollstonecraft was born the second of seven children. Her parents' marriage was unhappy and she often took care of her sisters and brothers. From an early age, Mary knew that women did not have the same opportunities as men. She received a poor education and left home at 18, supporting herself and often the family as a badly paid governess or teacher, the only occupation available to women of her class.

After her mother died, Mary, with her sister, Eliza, and close friend, Fanny Blood, opened a girls' school but it failed. Encouraged by friends, she took the bold step of deciding to earn her living as a writer. By this time she was meeting and making friends with many people who held unusual or radical ideas, such as Tom Paine. In 1787 she published her first work, *Thoughts on the Education of Daughters*. In this book she proposed that girls should be given a much better education than was usual at the time. Other books followed.

In 1792 she published her best-known book, *A Vindication of the Rights of Women*. In this Mary asked passionately why men should be the decision-makers when women could do so just as well. She questioned a society that made women economically dependent on men, and an education system that taught women to be merely 'the toy of man'. She described marriage as 'legal

Women in the 18th century

Women in 18th century Britain had no legal rights. They could not own property, sign legal documents or vote. They were effectively the 'property' of their fathers first, and their husbands when they married. They did not even have legal rights over their children.

prostitution', the first feminist to use the phrase. She said women were not naturally weak; they were made so by being dependent on men.

Mary's book made an enormous stir – the press called her a 'hyena in petticoats'. She then moved to France to see the Revolution and had a romantic affair and a daughter, Fanny, with an American called Gilbert Imlay. Mary tried to commit suicide when he deserted her.

In 1797 she married William Godwin, a journalist and political thinker, but Wollstonecraft died from an infectious fever eleven days after giving birth to her second daughter, also called Mary. Her book, *Vindication*, went on to inspire countless feminists and is still read today. Her daughter grew up to be Mary Shelley, the author of *Frankenstein*.

WILLIAM WILBERFORCE
POLITICIAN AND
ANTI-SLAVERY CAMPAIGNER

BORN Hull, Yorkshire,
24 August 1759
DIED London,
29 July 1833

Between the 15th and 19th centuries, some 7 million Africans were transported across the Atlantic to be sold into slavery. England was a leading slave trading nation and many people grew rich and powerful as a result. William Wilberforce was to lead the campaign against this dreadful trade.

Wilberforce attended Oxford University, where he made friends with William Pitt, later to become prime minister. Wilberforce decided to enter politics and in 1780 was elected member of parliament for Hull. In 1784 he became an evangelical Christian. Shocked by the horrors of the slave trade, he pledged to help end it.

In 1788 he made his first public speech against the slave trade. With the support of other campaigners, he presented a bill to the House of Commons demanding an end to the trade. It was heavily defeated. For the next 19 years Wilberforce campaigned tirelessly, presenting an anti-slave trade bill to the Commons every year.

His commitment and strong Christian beliefs earned him and other Christian abolitionists the nickname 'the Saints'. Finally Wilberforce was successful. In

Anti-slavery movement

From the late 18th century a powerful anti-slavery movement emerged in Britain. As well as Wilberforce, anti-slavery campaigners included **THOMAS CLARKSON** (1760-1846), **GRANVILLE SHARPE** (1735-1813) and **JOSIAH WEDGWOOD** (1730-95). There were also women anti-slavery campaigners who formed their own societies. They included **ELIZABETH PEASE** (1807-97), **ANNE KNIGHT** (1781-1862) and **ELIZABETH HEYRICK** (1769-1831).

1807 his Abolition of the Slave Trade Bill became law and ended the slave trade in the British West Indies.

Slavery itself still needed to be abolished. Wilberforce carried on campaigning until ill-health forced him to retire from parliament in 1825. Others continued the work and in 1833, one month after Wilberforce died, the Slavery Abolition Act was passed, ending slavery throughout the British Empire.

> **William Wilberforce's efforts helped to bring about the end of slavery in the British Empire.**

ELIZABETH FRY
QUAKER PHILANTHROPIST AND PRISON REFORMER

BORN Norwich,
Norfolk, 21 May 1780
DIED Ramsgate, Kent,
12 October 1845

Elizabeth Fry devoted her life to prison reform; her work led to many improvements. She was the first woman to present evidence to the House of Commons.

Elizabeth Fry was born Elizabeth Gurney into a wealthy Quaker family. Her mother died when she was 12 and she helped care for the family. As a teenager, she was introduced to the ideas of people like Mary Wollstonecraft (see pages 12–13) and Tom Paine (see pages 10–11). In 1800 she married a Quaker banker, John Fry. She became a Quaker preacher in 1810.

Quaker networks

Englishman **GEORGE FOX** (1624-91) founded the Quakers, or Society of Friends, In the 17th century. A Protestant Christian group, Quakers believe in equal rights between men and women, have often been pacifists (against war) and have done much work with the poor. In the 1700s and 1800s they played a leading role in the anti-slavery movement and other reforms.

Like many wealthy women, Elizabeth Fry was brought up to help the poor and needy. In 1813 she visited the women's section of Newgate Prison in London. She was shocked when she saw 300 women and their children living in terrible cramped conditions, sleeping on straw-covered stone. From then on, she fought for improvements. She visited the prison regularly, provided clothes for women, set up a prison school and chapel, and introduced sewing and Bible classes.

In 1817 she and 11 others founded the Association for the Improvement of Female Prisoners in Newgate. Her brother-in-law, now a member of parliament, promoted her work in the House of Commons. She gave evidence to a parliamentary committee and in 1823 the Gaol Act was passed. It introduced wages for prison officers, women warders and chaplain visits.

Elizabeth Fry continued campaigning, even though she had a large family of her own. She set up a training school for nurses and opened shelters for the homeless.

Queen Victoria supported her work. When she died, a thousand people attended her funeral.

This engraving of Quaker Elizabeth Fry demonstrates her quiet determination.

WILLIAM LOVETT
CHARTIST AND REFORMER

BORN Newlyn,
Cornwall, 8 May 1800
DIED London,
8 August 1877

William Lovett was a leading political figure in the 19th century. He believed passionately in co-operation (people working together), votes for all men and the value of education. He helped to found Chartism, a mass movement for political reform.

William Lovett spent his life trying to introduce political reforms and improve conditions for working people.

Lovett was born into a fishing family. He received a basic education before being apprenticed to a rope-maker. In 1821 he went to London where he worked as a cabinet-maker. Lovett continued his education at evening classes held at the London Mechanics' Institute – a working-class, self-education organisation. He began to write political articles for working-class newspapers.

In 1831 Lovett refused to do military service. He said that because he had no vote, he would not serve. He was fined and his goods seized. By the late 1830s he was in the forefront of the campaign for parliamentary reform. In 1832 the first Reform Act had given the vote to property-owning middle-class men but working-class men had been ignored, while votes for women were hardly mentioned.

In 1836 Lovett, and trade union activist Francis Place (1771–1854), founded the London Working Men's Association (LWMA). Lovett wrote their manifesto, or main aims, which he called the People's Charter. It was a remarkable document, which included six demands (see panel), among them manhood suffrage (the vote for all men over the age of 21). Turned into a petition, it became the focus for Chartism, the largest working-class movement ever seen. More than 1 million people signed the petition to show their agreement.

Chartism

Chartism was a mass working-class movement between 1838 and 1848. Its six demands were: manhood suffrage (the vote for all men over 21 years of age); a secret ballot (so that each person's vote remained private); payment for members of parliament, so that working men could become involved; no property qualifications for members of parliament; equal-sized electoral districts; and annual parliaments. Parliament rejected the Charter, and sixty Chartists were transported (sent as prisoners) to Australia. However, all Chartist demands have now been introduced, except for annual parliaments.

Lovett was arrested in 1839 and charged with seditious libel (writing and spreading material encouraging rebellion against the government). For this, he was imprisoned for a year. During this time, the Charter was presented to parliament – and rejected. In 1840 Lovett, by now ill, was released from prison.

Lovett spent the rest of his life running his own bookshop, writing textbooks and his autobiography. In 1841 he founded the National Association for Promoting the Political and Social Improvement of the People, which lasted for 15 years and set up some mobile libraries. Lovett made no money from his ventures and died in poverty. 🏴

EDWIN CHADWICK
SOCIAL REFORMER AND CIVIL SERVANT

BORN Manchester, 24 January 1800
DIED Surrey, 6 July 1890

In the early part of the 19th century, cities and towns were unhealthy places. Thousands of people died every year from diseases such as cholera and typhus, caused by dirty drinking water and poor drainage. Edwin Chadwick produced the first government report into public health.

Chadwick studied law but became a civil servant. In 1834 he worked for the Poor Law Commission, helping to administer workhouses. A very practical man, he developed the idea of 'less eligibility', that life in the workhouse should be more unpleasant than the lowest form of work. He also proposed a national police force to prevent crime.

In 1838 he began researching everyday life in industrial towns. In 1842 he published his *Report into the Sanitary Conditions of the Labouring Population of Great Britain*, in which he described the appalling lack of drainage and sewage systems in industrial towns. Until this time, governments had been reluctant to deal with social issues, preferring to follow what was known as a *laissez-faire* (let it be) approach. Chadwick's report challenged this situation. He argued that the government could and should improve people's lives by improving living conditions. He also pointed out that a healthier population would work harder and cost less to support in the workhouses.

In 1848, largely due to Chadwick's pressure, parliament passed the first-ever Public Health Act. This set up local and central Boards of Health and enabled them to introduce better public health facilities. It was not completely effective

Sources of disease

Edwin Chadwick believed disease was caused by air pollution. British physician **DR JOHN SNOW** (1813–58) believed germs spread infectious diseases. In 1854 he traced the source of a cholera epidemic to a drinking well in Soho, London, into which raw sewage was seeping.

because it did not force local authorities
to tackle the problems, but it marked
the start of government responsibility for
public health.

*The work of Edwin
Chadwick helped
put public health
on the agenda of
the British
government.*

LORD SHAFTESBURY
PHILANTHROPIST AND FACTORY REFORMER

BORN London,
28 April 1801
DIED Folkestone, Kent,
1 October 1885

Working conditions for many in the early part of the Industrial Revolution were dreadful. Children worked long hours in factories and mines with little protection. Lord Shaftesbury took up their cause.

An engraving of Lord Shaftesbury. His work helped to protect children from harsh working conditions.

Philanthropists

Philanthropists are people who spend time helping others. Poverty, ill-health and suffering were widespread during Queen Victoria's reign. It was often down to philanthropists to highlight the problems and find solutions. Journalist **HENRY MAYHEW** (1812–87) interviewed some of the poorest people and published articles about their lives. In 1865, **WILLIAM** (1829–1912) and **CATHERINE** (1829–1912) **BOOTH** founded what became the Salvation Army to provide necessities for the needy. In the 1890s, **CHARLES BOOTH** (1840–1916) and **SEEBOHM ROWNTREE** (1871–1954) produced reports showing that at least 20% of Britons did not have enough to eat.

Lord Shaftesbury was born Anthony Ashley Cooper, the eldest son of the Earl of Shaftesbury. He inherited the title on the death of his father in 1851.

When he was 25 he became a member of parliament and began to take a keen interest in the lives of working children in Britain. In 1833 he put forward a parliamentary bill proposing that working hours for children be reduced to ten hours a day. The bill was rejected. Children were cheap to employ and factory and mine owners thought that they would make less money if working conditions were changed. But the evidence Shaftesbury provided was so shocking that the government realised they had to protect children. So, later the same year, a Factory Act was passed making it illegal for children under the age of nine to work in textile mills.

Shaftesbury now turned his attention to the mines. He helped to set up an inquiry into children's employment in mines and collieries. The resulting report in 1842 made shocking reading. Children as young as four were working underground for at least 12 hours a day, opening and closing heavy trap doors to allow coal carts through, and older children were crawling through tunnels hauling coal carts behind them. The report was the first illustrated government report and it horrified Victorian society. After this, Shaftesbury persuaded parliament to pass the 1842 Mines Act, which banned the use of women and children underground.

Although some factory and mine owners continued to employ young children, Lord Shaftesbury made people start to question whether it was right to treat children in this way. Further factory acts followed, bringing in greater changes. Shaftesbury also showed interest in the education of working-class children and helped to set up many schools.

FLORENCE NIGHTINGALE
FOUNDER OF MODERN NURSING

BORN Florence, Italy,
12 May 1820
DIED London,
13 August 1910

Florence Nightingale was a remarkable and determined woman. Against all odds, she reformed nursing and made it an acceptable profession for middle-class women.

Florence was born into a wealthy family. In her late teens, she felt God had chosen her to do great work. Her life as a well-brought up 'lady' irritated her and she wrote in her diary that her days were boring and meaningless.

Despite pressure from her mother, she refused to marry and announced that she wanted to be a nurse, a job that only working-class women did at the time. Her parents were horrified but finally allowed her to train at a nursing school in Germany. On returning to London, she became superintendent of a women's hospital.

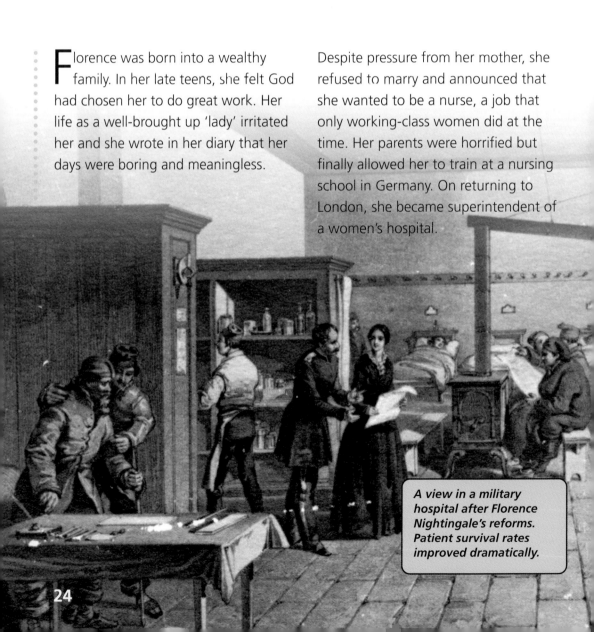

A view in a military hospital after Florence Nightingale's reforms. Patient survival rates improved dramatically.

In 1853, the Crimean War broke out with the British, French, Turkish and Sardinian armies fighting against the Russians. *The Times* newspaper reported that wounded British soldiers were dying in their thousands. Florence Nightingale volunteered to go to the Crimea to investigate. She was finally given permission and left for Turkey with 38 nurses. The conditions she found at the army hospital in Scutari were dreadful. Wounded men were lying in filth, without blankets or decent food, their wounds untreated. Despite opposition from the military, Nightingale reorganised the barracks, cleaned up the hospital and introduced proper nursing. Death rates dropped dramatically.

In 1856, Nightingale returned to Britain, a heroine. She campaigned to improve

Medical pioneers

Other 19th century women who made their mark in medicine were Jamaican nurse **MARY SEACOLE** (1805–81), who overcame racism as well as sexism, **SOPHIA JEX-BLAKE** (1840–1912), who opened a medical school for women in Edinburgh, and **ELIZABETH GARRETT ANDERSON** (1836–1917), the first English woman doctor.

nursing conditions in all military hospitals and gave evidence to the House of Commons that led to the setting up of the Army Medical College. With money from wealthy friends, she founded the Nightingale School and Home for Nurses at St Thomas' Hospital, London, and wrote a major nursing textbook.

JOSEPHINE BUTLER
SOCIAL REFORMER

BORN
Northumberland,
13 April 1828
DIED Northumberland,
30 December 1906

Josephine Butler campaigned against the abuse of women, especially prostitutes, at a time when women hardly talked about sex. She successfully argued for changes to the law.

Josephine was born Josephine Grey to an upper middle-class family. Her parents campaigned against slavery, and she grew up surrounded by politics and talk of fairness and equality for all. In 1852 she married a headmaster, George Butler. They moved to Liverpool and had four children. In 1863 their six-year-old daughter died in an accident. Struggling to cope with the tragedy, Josephine turned to charity work, especially with prostitutes. Prostitutes are women who offer sex for money. Some of the prostitutes were very young and Josephine was horrified at how men treated them.

In 1864 the government passed the first of three Contagious Diseases Acts. They were intended to stop the spread of syphilis (a sexually-transmitted disease) in the armed forces. Any woman living in a military town suspected of being a 'common prostitute' could be arrested, medically examined and locked up if she resisted or had the disease.

Josephine Butler believed the Acts were unjust. They punished women for being prostitutes, but not the men who used them and spread the disease. In 1869 she launched a massive campaign. With other women she formed the Ladies National Association (LNA). They presented a petition, which shocked members of parliament, all of whom were men. Josephine travelled throughout the country speaking out against the Acts and encouraging women to resist. She spoke in the House of Commons and started her own newspaper to publicise her cause. Her campaigning shocked many people but also gained support. In 1886 the Acts were withdrawn.

Josephine also campaigned against child prostitution and fought against the so-called 'white slave trade', which sold young women into prostitution. She argued that working-class women should receive a better education and job opportunities.

Josephine Butler in old age. Her campaign helped to protect women from abuse.

ANNIE BESANT
JOURNALIST AND CAMPAIGNER FOR BIRTH CONTROL

BORN London,
1 October 1847
DIED India,
20 September, 1933

Annie Besant campaigned for birth control when it was still a taboo subject, and championed the cause of young working-class women.

Annie was born Annie Wood. She married a clergyman when she was 19 and they had two children. However, she was unhappy and left the marriage, taking her daughter with her.

Annie formed a friendship with Charles Bradlaugh, editor of a radical journal, the *National Reformer,* and wrote regular articles on women and marriage. In 1877 she and Bradlaugh reprinted an old pamphlet, *The Fruits of Philosophy*, which argued that birth control should be made available. They were accused of publishing disgusting literature and given prison sentences, although these were not carried through. Not put off, Besant wrote her own book promoting birth control, *The Laws of Population*. Many people read it and newspapers accused her of writing filth. On the strength of this, her husband took her daughter away to live with him.

Annie Besant became a socialist and started her own newspaper, *The Link*. In 1888 she wrote about the match girls, young women who worked for the Bryant & May match factory in Bow, East London. She drew attention to their low pay and dangerous working conditions, caused by inhaling phosphorus fumes. When three of the match girls who talked to Annie Besant were sacked, Annie helped them form a union. After a three-week strike, the match girls won better pay and conditions, and the three women were re-employed.

Married Love

Another British woman who campaigned for birth control was **MARIE STOPES** (1880–1958). In 1921 she opened Britain's first family planning clinic in London. She also wrote Britain's first book of sexual advice. It was called *Married Love* and was published in 1918. Thousands of ordinary women and men wrote letters thanking her.

Later, Annie Besant turned to theosophy, a mystical movement. She went to India where she joined the fight for Indian independence.

This photograph of Annie Besant captures her direct and forceful personality.

JAMES KEIR HARDIE
FIRST LABOUR MEMBER OF PARLIAMENT

BORN Lanarkshire, Scotland, 15 August 1856
DIED 26 September 1915

James Keir Hardie spent his life fighting for working-class people. He felt they needed their own political party and founded the Independent Labour Party, the forerunner of the Labour Party.

Hardie was born into extreme poverty. His mother was a domestic servant and single parent. When he was seven, Hardie started working as an errand boy. At the age of ten, he went to work down the mines. He had no formal schooling but his mother taught him to read and he went to night school after work.

A staunch socialist, Hardie helped to set up a miners' union, and, in 1880, led the first miners' strike in Lanarkshire. He was sacked as a result. He became secretary of the Scottish Miners' Federation and started his own newspaper, *The Miner*.

Working-class men had gained the vote in 1884 but there was no working-class political party. The only choices were the Liberals or Tories. In 1886, backed by the miners, Hardie stood for parliament as an independent socialist candidate. He failed to win the seat but from this point on, he worked to create a new political party. In 1892 he stood for parliament again, this time as an independent Labour candidate. He succeeded and entered the House of Commons wearing a cloth cap and tweed suit, Britain's first socialist member of parliament. (Other members of parliament wore top hats and long coats.)

Hardie campaigned for socialist policies: higher taxes for the rich, old age pensions, schools for working-class people and the abolition of the House of Lords. In 1893 he helped form a socialist group: the Independent Labour Party (ILP). As leader of the ILP he worked to bring trade unions and socialist groups together to create one large political party. In 1900 the Labour Representation Committee (LRC) was founded. By 1906, it had become the Labour Party. It won 29 seats and Hardie was elected head of the party. In 1910, 40 Labour members of parliament were elected to the House of Commons.

Hardie remained a member of parliament until 1915. A pacifist, he opposed the Boer War and World War I.

This poster for the 1910 General Election features a portrait of James Keir Hardie.

EMMELINE PANKHURST
SUFFRAGETTE

BORN Manchester,
14 July 1858
DIED London,
14 June 1928

Between 1906 and 1914, thousands of British women fought an intense battle to win votes for women. One of their most famous leaders was Emmeline Pankhurst. With her daughters, Christabel and Sylvia, she inspired and led an extraordinary campaign.

Police manhandle Mrs Pankhurst, removing her forcibly from a demonstration.

Women had been asking for the vote since at least the 1860s, without success. They had relied on male friends in the House of Commons to demand change. Emmeline Pankhurst decided that this was never going to work and so, in 1903, she founded the Women's Social and Political Union (WSPU) in Manchester. Its aim was to get votes for women immediately, by any means necessary. It rejected co-operation with government in favour of being disruptive and using force. The WSPU made headline news when Christabel Pankhurst and Annie Kenney were arrested at a Liberal Party election meeting for standing up and demanding votes for women.

From then on the WSPU was rarely out of the news. Emmeline and her daughter, Christabel, now living in London, ran the WSPU like an army, calling on their supporters to take ever more dramatic action. Emmeline encouraged WSPU members — nicknamed suffragettes in 1906 — to heckle (shout at) members of parliament, demonstrate and hold mass meetings. Week after week, suffragettes charged at the House of Commons in an attempt to gain entry. The police responded brutally, by punching and kicking the suffragettes.

Mrs Millicent Fawcett

MRS MILLICENT FAWCETT (1847–1929) was another leading campaigner for votes for women. She led the National Union of Women's Suffrage Society (NUWSS) from 1897–1919. Unlike Pankhurst, Mrs Fawcett did not support the use of force.

Emmeline was arrested several times. From 1909 she and many others went on hunger strike in prison. The government's reaction was to force-feed them, a brutal process that shocked many. As the years dragged on, suffragette activity became increasingly forceful and lost much public support.

In 1914 World War I began. Emmeline stopped her campaign and urged women to work for the war effort. It split the movement as some suffragettes were against all war. However, during the war, women replaced men in many jobs and, in 1918, the law changed to give property-owning women over the age of 30 the vote. In 1928 women over 21 achieved the vote on equal terms with men.

ELEANOR RATHBONE
FEMINIST, SOCIAL REFORMER AND POLITICIAN

BORN Liverpool,
12 May 1872
DIED 2 January 1946

Eleanor Rathbone was one of the greatest women members of parliament of the 20th century. She campaigned on many social issues: poverty, women's rights and refugees. One of her greatest achievements was to secure family allowances, known today as child benefit.

Educated at Oxford University, Eleanor Rathbone took an early interest in poverty and on women's dependence on men for money. In 1909 she became the first woman to be elected to Liverpool City Council, a position she held until 1934, and in 1929 she was elected to the House of Commons as an independent member of parliament.

During World War 1 (1914–18), Eleanor Rathbone had set up a committee to examine poverty in Britain. She and her colleagues published *Equal Pay and the Family*, a report in which she argued for the introduction of family allowances. She wrote two more publications on the subject, *The Disinherited Family* (1924) and *The Case for Family Allowances* (1940). Eleanor Rathbone believed passionately that women should be paid an allowance for children so that they would not have to be entirely dependent on their husbands for money, and so that men could no longer claim higher wages than women on the grounds of supporting a family. It took nearly 30 years, against considerable opposition, for her to achieve this aim. Family allowances were finally introduced in 1945, the year before she died.

Eleanor Rathbone took a keen interest in foreign affairs. She campaigned for women's rights in India, as well as in Britain, and was one of the first members of parliament to highlight the dangers of Nazi Germany. In 1939 she set up a parliamentary committee to

The welfare state

From 1942 the British government drew up proposals for a welfare state, which came into force after World War II (1939–45). The Family Allowances Act, for which Eleanor Rathbone had campaigned, was a major achievement. Another was the National Health Service (NHS).

Eleanor Rathbone was a tireless campaigner for family allowances.

investigate the fate of minorities in fascist countries. She also encouraged the government to take up individual cases, particularly of Jewish refugees. 🇬🇧

ELLEN WILKINSON
SOCIALIST AND POLITICIAN

BORN Manchester,
8 October 1891
DIED London,
6 February 1947

Known as 'Red Ellen' because of her fiery red hair and left-wing views, Ellen Wilkinson fought for the unemployed. She also introduced important laws on hire purchase and school milk.

Socialism attracted Ellen Wilkinson from an early age. When she was 16 she joined the Independent Labour Party (ILP). In 1923 she was elected to Manchester City Council and was Labour member of parliament for Middlesborough East from 1924 to 1931. In 1933 she became member of parliament for Jarrow, on Tyneside.

Ellen Wilkinson takes a break with some of the Jarrow marchers in 1936.

The 1930s was a hard time in Britain as many people lost their jobs and so struggled to feed and clothe their families. Jarrow was particularly hard hit with about 80 per cent unemployment. In 1936 Ellen Wilkinson organised what became an historic march, leading 200 unemployed workers from Jarrow to London — a distance of about 451 km. The aim was to find jobs for Jarrow people and to highlight the misery of mass unemployment. Marchers walked with banners and were helped by people along the way who provided food and places to sleep. Nearly a month after starting, the marchers arrived in London. Ellen Wilkinson, as their member of parliament, handed a petition of 12,000 signatures into parliament. Parliament did little for Jarrow but the march gained enormous publicity.

Ellen Wilkinson was always aware of the difficulties facing ordinary people. In 1938 she introduced a Hire Purchase Act to protect people who bought goods on hire purchase (credit). In 1945 she was appointed Minister of Education, the first woman to hold that post. Thanks to her efforts, free milk was offered to all schoolchildren under the age of 18.

Ellen Wilkinson remained member of parliament for Jarrow until her death. Tragically, she suffered serious depression and eventually took her own life. Today, there are a number of schools in Britain named after her.

LORD DAVID PITT
DOCTOR AND CIVIL RIGHTS CAMPAIGNER

BORN Grenada,
3 October 1913
DIED London,
18 December 1994

In the years following World War II (1939–45), thousands of Caribbean men and women came to Britain to work. Although they were British citizens, they faced terrible racism and discrimination. Lord David Pitt fought to end that racism and promote equal rights for black Britons.

Pitt first came to Britain from the Caribbean in 1933 to study medicine at Edinburgh University. After qualifying he returned to the Caribbean and became active in the fight for Caribbean independence.

In 1947 Pitt returned to Britain. He set up a medical practice in London that he ran for 30 years. Combining medicine with politics he decided to challenge the widespread racism that existed in Britain. He joined the League of Coloured Peoples, which had been founded in 1933 to campaign for black people. From the 1960s he became a leading black campaigner. He helped immigrants and founded the Campaign against Racial Discrimination (CARD). His efforts to improve race relations helped to

Black Britons

Other black activists who campaigned against discrimination and for the rights of black Britons have included: **HAROLD MOODY** (1882–1947), the founder of the League of Coloured Peoples in 1931, the first effective black pressure group in Britain; **CLAUDIA JONES** (1915–64), founder of the *West Indian Gazette* and the Notting Hill Carnival; and **DIANE ABBOT** (b. 1953), first black woman member of parliament and founder of Black Women Mean Business.

Lord David Pitt, photographed in front of Westminster Bridge and the Houses of Parliament.

shape the landmark Race Relations Act of 1976, which made racial discrimination illegal in housing, jobs, training, education and social services. It was a major victory. The Act also set up the Commission for Racial Equality (CRE), still in existence today.

Pitt stood for parliament twice – in 1959 and 1970. Each time he experienced racism and failed to win. He was elected to the London County Council (LCC), later the Greater London Council (GLC), and helped to shape its anti-racist policies. In 1975 he was appointed to the House of Lords and in 1985 became the first black president of the British Medical Association (BMA).

BRUCE KENT
PACIFIST AND ANTI-WAR CAMPAIGNER

BORN London, 22 June 1929

Bruce Kent is probably Britain's best-known peace campaigner. Since the 1950s, he has campaigned against nuclear weapons and for an end to war.

Educated at Catholic school and in Canada, Bruce Kent did military service as an officer in the Royal Tank Regiment during the late 1940s. He studied law at Oxford University and was ordained as a Catholic priest in 1958. He went on to be a chaplain at London University and a parish priest.

Bruce Kent first became involved in the peace movement in 1958. He joined Pax Christi, an international Catholic peace organisation, and became increasingly involved in campaigning against war, and nuclear weapons in particular. In 1958, the Campaign for Nuclear Disarmament (CND) was founded to work for an end to nuclear weapons. Bruce Kent became an active member. Support for CND declined during the 1970s but rose again during the early 1980s when nuclear cruise missiles were stationed in Britain. Bruce Kent became CND's general secretary in 1980 and served as CND's chair from 1987-90.

In 1987 Cardinal Hume, then Archbishop of Westminster, told Bruce Kent to end his political activities. Hume felt they did not fit with his duties as a priest. Bruce Kent refused and resigned his priesthood. In 1992 he stood unsuccessfully as Labour Party candidate for Oxford. Since then he has continued his anti-war activities, broadcasting and addressing meetings. He has taken an interest in peace education and most recently founded his own organisation, Movement for Abolition of War, 'to get people to realise that war is not an essential part of civilisation'.

Peace campaigners

For as long as there have been wars, there have been anti-war campaigners. CND's founders included **DORA** (1894–1986) and **BERTRAND** (1872–1970) **RUSSELL** and Labour member of parliament **FENNER BROCKWAY** (1888–1988). In 1981 some women set up a peace camp at Greenham Common, where American cruise missiles were held.

Peace campaigner
Bruce Kent (front)
photographed during a
protest at Greenham
Common airbase in
the 1980s.

JONATHON PORRITT
ENVIRONMENTAL CAMPAIGNER AND WRITER

BORN London,
6 July 1950

Most people today are worried about environmental threats, such as global warming, pollution and nuclear power. But it was not always so. One campaigner who has brought these issues to the forefront is Jonathon Porritt.

After studying at Oxford University, Porritt worked as an English teacher. He was interested in environmental concerns and joined the Ecology Party, which had been formed in 1973. Under his leadership (1978–84), membership of and support for the Ecology Party grew rapidly.

In 1979 the party put up 50 candidates in the general election. In 1983 this had grown to more than 100 Ecology Party candidates. They polled 40,000 votes but won no seats. By 1978 the Ecology Party had become today's Green Party.

Porritt published his first book, *Seeing Green*, in 1984. It was a landmark book that put the case for green politics. He gave up teaching and from 1984–90 was director of Friends of the Earth, an environmental campaigning group, which drew attention to the destruction of habitats and the dangers of pollution.

Porritt left Friends of the Earth to concentrate on writing and broadcasting. He wanted to focus on practical solutions to environmental problems. In 1996, with environmentalists Sara Parkin and Paul Ekins, he founded Forum for the Future, an environmental charity that aims to find ways of achieving sustainable development.

He has also been environmental adviser to the government, businesses and Prince Charles. In 2000 he was appointed Chairman of the UK Sustainable Development Commission and awarded a CBE. In 2005, he caused a stir with his new book *Capitalism as if the World Matters*, which offers ways in which capitalism can be re-invented to minimise its environmental impact.

Porritt remains a member of the Green Party. He does not own a car but travels by bicycle and train. He is critical of the UK's record on the environment. 🇬🇧

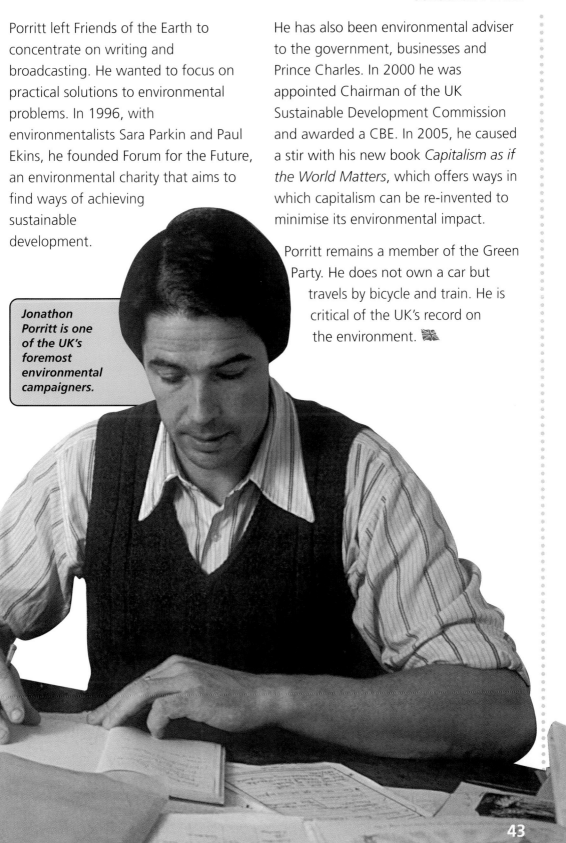

Jonathon Porritt is one of the UK's foremost environmental campaigners.

SHAMI CHAKRABATI
LAWYER AND HUMAN RIGHTS CAMPAIGNER

BORN London, 16 June 1969

Since the beginning of the 21st century, there has been an increasing anxiety about global terrorism. As anti-terrorism laws are introduced to the UK, Shami Chakrabati has campaigned to make sure that human rights and civil liberties are not at risk.

Shami Chakrabati studied at the London School of Economics. From 1996–2001 she was a barrister (a type of lawyer) at the Home Office, concerned with issues of asylum and counter-terrorism laws. In September 2001 she joined Liberty, one of the leading human rights and civil liberties organisations in the UK. She took up her post just one day before the 9/11 attacks on the United States, when terrorists flew planes into the World Trade Center and the Pentagon. In 2003, she became Liberty's director.

Following the 9/11 attacks, Shami Chakrabati focused her attention on the threat to human rights and civil liberties caused by anti-terrorism laws being introduced into Britain. While recognising the dangers of terrorism, she has campaigned against the introduction of identity cards (ID cards), on the grounds that they infringe individual freedoms such as the right to privacy. She has also highlighted the threat to civil liberties of many of the anti-terrorist measures introduced by the government, such as extra powers for the police and extending the period of time in which suspects can be detained. Since 2003 Shami Chakrabati has contributed to many media debates

Father of human rights

PETER BENENSON (1921–2005) has been described as the 'father of human rights'. In 1961, after reading about the plight of two students jailed in fascist Portugal for drinking a toast to liberty, he founded Amnesty International to campaign for political prisoners. Today Amnesty is one of the most influential human rights organisations.

and has warned that new anti-terror laws could fall foul of the UN Charter of Human Rights. In 2006 she was shortlisted for Channel 4's Political Award for the 'Most Inspiring Political Figure'. Following a public vote, she came second, after TV chef Jamie Oliver but beating Prime Minister Tony Blair. 🏴

Shami Chakrabati photographed outside the High Court on the Strand in London.

Glossary

Abolitionist Someone who campaigned for the abolition (ending) of slavery.

Asylum Seeking safety in another country to avoid persecution at home.

Bill The draft of a proposed new law, which is presented to parliament. If the bill is passed, it becomes an act of parliament.

Chartism A mass working-class movement for political reform that lasted from 1838-48.

Civil liberties Basic personal rights of the individual, guaranteed by law.

Colony A country or area that is ruled by another country.

Class Social grouping, as in working-class, middle-class, upper-class.

Crimean War The war fought between Russia and the allied powers of England, France, Turkey and Sardinia over control of the Balkans in southeast Europe (1853–65).

Democracy Government by the people for the people. In practice, a political system like the British system where people vote for political candidates who will represent them.

Ecology The study of living things and their relationship with their environment or surroundings.

English Civil War The conflict (1642-49) between Charles I and his supporters, and the parliamentarians over who should have the greatest say in the government of England. It was a bitter struggle that ended with the execution of the King and the establishment of a republic under Oliver Cromwell. In 1660 the monarchy was restored.

Environmentalist Someone who is concerned with protecting the natural environment.

Feminist Someone who believes in and promotes women's rights.

Green politics Politics with environmental issues at their heart.

Green Party Political party that campaigns on green issues. Formerly the Ecology Party.

Heresy An opinion or belief that contradicts or challenges established religious teachings.

Holy Communion Christian ceremony in which worshippers receive bread or a wafer and wine, representing the body and blood of Jesus Christ, or the Last Supper. Wycliffe criticised this ceremony saying it was not real. At the time this was considered heresy.

Human rights The rights we have or think we should have because we are human, for instance, the right to a fair trial or freedom from discrimination. In 1948 the United Nations published its Charter of Human Rights.

Industrial Revolution Name given to the huge industrial and technological changes that took place in Britain between about 1760-1830.

Labour Party Political party created by socialists and trade unions to represent the working class. Developed from the Independent Labour Party (1900) and took the name Labour Party in 1906.

Liberals Members of the Liberal Party (formerly Whigs). During the 19th century, the Liberal Party represented business people and industrialists.

Monarchy A ruling royal family. A monarch is a king or queen.

Pacifist Someone who is totally opposed to war.

Philanthropist A person who does charitable work and/or uses his or her money to do charitable work, usually with the poor and needy.

Puritan A part of the Church of England in the 17th century which wanted radical reform.

Quaker Member of a Christian group, the Society of Friends.

Racism Prejudice about one particular racial or ethnic group. Usually a belief that whites are superior to blacks.

Radical Someone who believes in sweeping economic, social or political changes. Can be used to describe the changes themselves.

Reformation A movement for reform of the Roman Catholic Church. It began in what is now Germany in the early 1500s.

Republic A country without a royal family, which is ruled by elected representatives.

Revolutionary Someone who believes that change can only come about by overthrowing an existing system.

Sedition Speech or action encouraging rebellion.

Sexism Discrimination against one sex.

Socialism A political system that believes in public ownership of industry, transport and other resources.

Suffrage The right to vote.

Sustainable economics The idea that we should live and work in such a way that we do not damage the environment.

Taboo Something that cannot be talked about because it is against society's rules or beliefs.

Tories Members of the Tory Party, forerunner of today's Conservative Party.

Workhouse In the 1800s, places where the unemployed, poor and elderly were forced to live if they couldn't work.

Some useful websites

http://www.spartacus.schoolnet.co.uk
A good starting point to find out more about people who campaigned to reform parliament.

http://www.spartacus.schoolnet.co.uk/slavery.html
Information on the slave trade and the abolitionists.

http://www.bbc.co.uk/history/trail/victorian_britain/
Information on all aspects of Victorian Britain.

http://www.100greatblackbritons.com/news.html
Biographies of 100 famous black Britons.

http://www.bbc.co.uk/radio4/womanshour/timeline/timelines.html
Women's history timeline (audio)

Note to parents and teachers:
Every effort has been made by the Publishers to ensure that the websites in this book are suitable for children, that they are of the highest educational value, and that they contain no inappropriate or offensive material. However, because of the nature of the Internet, it is impossible to guarantee that the contents of these sites will not be altered. We strongly advise that Internet access is supervised by a responsible adult.

SOME PLACES TO VISIT

Bull House, High Street, Lewes, East Sussex
Home to Tom Paine for six years. Lewes holds a Tom Paine project festival every 4-14 July.

Wilberforce House, High Street, Hull, Yorkshire
Birthplace of William Wilberforce, now a museum. Includes information on slavery and the slave trade.

The Florence Nightingale Museum, St Thomas' Hospital, 2 Lambeth Palace Road, London, SE1 7EW
Contains information about Florence Nightingale and exhibitions on related topics, such as Mary Seacole.

The People's History Museum, Bridge Street Manchester M3 3ER
Contains trade union banners, Chartist and Labour Party archives and lots more information about working-class history and movements.

The Women's Library, London Metropolitan University, Old Castle Street, London, E1 7NT
Houses the Josephine Butler collection and other material about campaigning women, including the suffragettes.

House of Commons, Westminster, London
Contains a bronze bust of James Keir Hardie.

Index

These are the lists of contents for each title in *Great Britons*:

LEADERS
Boudica • Alfred the Great • Richard I • Edward I • Robert Bruce
Owain Glyndwr • Henry V • Henry VIII • Elizabeth I
Oliver Cromwell • The Duke of Marlborough • Robert Walpole
Horatio Nelson • Queen Victoria • Benjamin Disraeli
William Gladstone • David Lloyd George • Winston Churchill
Clement Attlee • Margaret Thatcher

CAMPAIGNERS FOR CHANGE
John Wycliffe • John Lilburne • Thomas Paine • Mary Wollstonecraft
William Wilberforce • Elizabeth Fry • William Lovett
Edwin Chadwick • Lord Shaftesbury • Florence Nightingale
Josephine Butler • Annie Besant • James Keir Hardie • Emmeline Pankhurst
Eleanor Rathbone • Ellen Wilkinson • Lord David Pitt • Bruce Kent
Jonathon Porritt • Shami Chakrabati

NOVELISTS
Aphra Behn • Jonathan Swift • Henry Fielding • Jane Austen
Charles Dickens • The Brontë Sisters • George Eliot • Lewis Carroll
Thomas Hardy • Robert Louis Stevenson • Arthur Conan Doyle
Virginia Woolf • D H Lawrence • J R R Tolkien • George Orwell
Graham Greene • William Golding • Ian McEwan • J K Rowling
Caryl Phillips • Andrea Levy • Zadie Smith
Monica Ali • Salman Rushdie

ARTISTS
Nicholas Hilliard • James Thornhill • William Hogarth
Joshua Reynolds • George Stubbs • William Blake • J M W Turner
John Constable • David Wilkie • Dante Gabriel Rossetti
Walter Sickert • Gwen John • Wyndham Lewis • Vanessa Bell
Henry Moore • Barbara Hepworth • Francis Bacon • David Hockney
Anish Kapoor • Damien Hirst

ENGINEERS
Robert Hooke • Abraham Darby • James Watt • John MacAdam
Thomas Telford • George Cayley • George Stephenson • Robert Stephenson
Joseph Paxton • Isambard Kingdom Brunel • Henry Bessemer
Joseph Bazalgette • Joseph Whitworth • Charles Parsons • Henry Royce
Nigel Gresley • Lord Nuffield • Harry Ricardo • Frank Whittle • Norman Foster

SCIENTISTS
John Dee • Robert Boyle • Isaac Newton • Edmond Halley • William Herschel
Michael Faraday • Charles Babbage • Mary Anning • Charles Darwin
Lord Kelvin • James Clerk Maxwell • Ernest Rutherford • Joseph Rotblat
Dorothy Hodgkin • Alan Turing • Francis Crick • Stephen Hawking
John Sulston • Jocelyn Bell Burnell • Susan Greenfield

SPORTING HEROES
WG Grace • Arthur Wharton • Kitty Godfree • Roger Bannister
Stirling Moss • Jackie Stewart • Bobby Moore • George Best
Gareth Edwards • Barry Sheene • Ian Botham • Nick Faldo
Torville and Dean • Lennox Lewis • Daley Thompson • Steve Redgrave
Tanni Grey-Thompson • Kelly Holmes • David Beckham • Ellen McArthur

MUSICIANS
William Byrd • Henry Purcell • George Frideric Handel • Arthur Sullivan
Edward Elgar • Henry Wood • Ralph Vaughan Williams • Noel Coward
Michael Tippet • Benjamin Britten • Vera Lynn
John Dankworth and Cleo Laine • Jacqueline Du Pre
Eric Clapton • Andrew Lloyd Webber • Elvis Costello
Simon Rattle • The Beatles • Courtney Pine • Evelyn Glennie